A MAD SEA

RANDY MASCORRO

Copyright © 2018 Rad Press Publishing

Randy Mascorro

"A Mad Sea"

All rights reserved. No part of this publication may be reproduced, distributed or conveyed without the permission of the author.

Cover & Interior design by: Mitch Green

A MAD SEA

If you find me

in the dark

remind me

that tiredness

can still be the sun

and my worry

can still be

serenity.

My days

can still hinder

and my voice

won't always

tell the truth.

RANDY MASCORRO

Because
what I admire
is not
what others admire.
What I want
is to see you
and I can start
peeling off
my layers.
You can start
undressing
your thoughts
and we can
make something
of these
tragic days.

A MAD SEA

Can we sleep?
Can we be here
and sink into
these sheets?
Now,
I have heard
time is a friend
but let's stop
every clock
and bend
every rule.
Let's laugh
at the thought
that we ever
have to be
found.

RANDY MASCORRO

Any road

can lead

to any heart,

and the

days will

shorten.

I fear

signs

on the windows

stay the same;

people just

change.

I heard a city

is more lonely

than a town.

Oh,

the lights

scream and plead.

We disappear into

each other.

We disappear into

each other.

A MAD SEA

If we lay ourselves down
and stretch out
all these worries
would we stay?
If we saw all that we are
spilled in front of us
would we want to touch
each other?
This skin
with trouble
scribbled everywhere,
we have memories
engraved on us.
We have cuts on our hands
from trusting
the same knife.

RANDY MASCORRO

Count
the sunflowers
and kiss me
twice.
Can I take
your hand
and remember
what it felt
like
to not freeze?
Can I inhale
your energy?

A MAD SEA

Can we describe our favorite

moment,

and every time

we have had

our smiles

burned alive?

Can we describe

something we can't

quite explain?

Or maybe

how deep this cut is

and how it feels

to truly

bleed

from the

past?

RANDY MASCORRO

If our stories
become skin
can our hands
finish a chapter?
And if my eyes
become hidden
will I recognize
who I am?
The hours
sleep
with the minutes.
Weary days
shatter
into weeks.
The seconds
scream,
the
seconds
scream.

A MAD SEA

Maybe one day
I can shred
these feelings
into the sea.
Maybe one day
I can see myself
clearly in the tide.
I can wrap
all my mistakes
around me,
and the cry
of the breeze will know
that even storms
settle
eventually.

RANDY MASCORRO

Turn down
the volume.
Let's remove
the shield
we are wearing.
Let's engrave
this moment
in our skin.
And for once
flowers bloom
from the sight
of us.

A MAD SEA

I have grown

tired

of my heart

not fitting right.

All these words,

all these uneven

skies.

Feed me to

the wolves.

Throw me

to the

rebels;

and the ones

who have gone mad.

RANDY MASCORRO

I'll find you
between the stars
with your glittery eyes
and your storyteller skin.
I will find you
in dreams
where time
does not chase us,
and we will survive
on elation.

A MAD SEA

If I told the sea
my troubles
would she listen
while I wept?
Can I put myself
in saltwater,
wipe away
all these years,
all this
lost time?
Can I tell
the waves
I am sorry
for not
realizing
how deep
forgiveness
is?

RANDY MASCORRO

The cosmic stars
are falling,
can you see them?
Can you see
changes in our eyes,
and how we glow
so freely?
Can I see them?
Can I see how our
questions
never yawn,
but
answers
sleep loudly?
Can we both
look through
the air
and laugh?
Look through
the air
and laugh?

A MAD SEA

If time

is a mirror

let me shatter

it to pieces.

Let me crash into

right now

and sever

what I don't know.

I will open

my skin

from every

inch of

every reflection

of myself.

RANDY MASCORRO

From the depths
of my ocean breath
I never struggle
to take you in.
How can a torch
and water be?
How can this flame
wrap who they are
around something
so ever changing?
If this is
how it truly feels
to melt,
I am more than happy
to be rain
after the fire.

A MAD SEA

Can I make you
a playlist
of every song I am.
Can I wrap it
in a letter
and give it
to you in winter?
Can you keep it sealed
and open it
on the coldest day?
Can I remember
that I still
have warmth,
even in the most
frigid times?

RANDY MASCORRO

Tell me again
how we crossed
bridges
we should of
never
walked over.
And our fingertips
have felt things
that feel things,
that feel like home.
A person.
A place.
A story.
A face.
Have you ever
had a song
play in your eyes
when you look
at someone
you love?

A MAD SEA

If I ripped out
my past
and pressed it
against my chest,
could I still breathe?
Could I still remember
moments that have
shaped me,
moments
that darkness
does not
want back?
Can I make
a pact with
the sun
and shake hands
with everything
that hurts.

RANDY MASCORRO

Can we read
each other
not from
start to finish?
Can we stop
in the middle?
Can you look at me
and see who I am?
This way,
see that I am
no longer
chasing the days
and I am okay
being still.
Can I look at you
and see who you are?
This way,
see that you
give this life
a paranormal
gift
in your
supernatural
skin.

A MAD SEA

I am struggling

to find balance.

If life is a war

my mind

is a battlefield.

I will

plant flowers

in the dirt

and soon

a new smile

will bloom.

RANDY MASCORRO

I am burning

for the sea.

Can I please

just cover up

with the waves

and remember how

it felt

to breathe?

I am burning

for the sea.

A MAD SEA

I haven't said much
but my eyes still hear you.
My voice
still screams for you.
Maybe the air holds the past.
We don't even look for it.
Memories become a drag.
Cigarettes burn faster
than us.
We drift.
We drift weeks and months,
even years.
Our souls wonder why
we can't fall into each other
like we used to.

RANDY MASCORRO

Lay
here in forgiveness
with me.
We can ditch
all the sorrow
we wear,
and donate
all the trouble
we speak.
Lay
here in forgiveness
with me.
Both our eyes
will shine new,
both our eyes
will shine new.

A MAD SEA

If time
yelled
out
from a
passing
car
would we hear it?
If we tore
every fear
off of
us
would we
feel it?
How do we
go deaf
from so
many memories?
And how can
we
go numb
from so
many
mistakes?

RANDY MASCORRO

Ends

and

beginnings.

Fingertips lie,

and what we believe

what we touch

is ours.

A MAD SEA

Please never

tell me

what my eyes

have seen.

I have never

grasped

what you have

felt.

We hold up

the world differently.

You

and I,

but

baby

we still

burn the same.

Find me
in the corners
of my mind
where the edge
is worth going over.
Where silence
says all the things
we can't
say.
Find me here
with ripped up
letters
I sent to myself.
Find me
in the corners
where time
plays dead,
and we hide.
We hide

A MAD SEA

If I held

my hands

out to you

could you see

who you are

in me?

Could you see

poison

and freedom?

Oh,

how quickly

a human

can kill us,

and how fast

a human

can take us

places

we have never

been.

RANDY MASCORRO

I don't know
what I am
doing.
That
is the exciting
part.
Our skin
over the bones
that fight
for us.
How can we
not chase
ourselves?
And who says
that we ever
have to be caught?

A MAD SEA

If you saw
beneath this frame
that holds me
together,
would you
recognize
everything
that did not fit,
and every lost
piece
of who I am?
Could I see
what I feel?
Could I strip
away houses
of myself,
and explain to you
how it felt
to live in every
single one.

If all

the stories

and pages

were cut,

would our words

still be in place?

If all this

fell away,

would all

the paragraphs

we bled over

find their

way back

to us?

A MAD SEA

Look me in my face,
let the minutes fade
and wash away like we have
let us hold these fears
in our hands.
We are afraid.
We are afraid to live
in this skin.
We are afraid.

And if fire

shouts up

from the

ground

I will silence

it

and send it

back down.

I will tell

the devil himself

that the flame

of herself

is all I see,

and the way

she burns

can soothe

the sea.

A MAD SEA

Now
before all
this mattered,
did time
pretend
to speak,
and did
all
the voices
we once
heard
fall away?
Can the hours
laugh
from every
stolen
second?

RANDY MASCORRO

I once told myself
to be more gentle
with my own
troubles,
remembering
there was forgiveness
buried somewhere
deep
in this skin.
I once told myself
to keep everyone
far
from me,
but I soon
realized
these silent
wounds
dance around,
and the piano
plays
my sins
perfectly.

A MAD SEA

When darkness
covers my mind,
it's our conversations
that bring
the sun
and when I rattle
with worry
I survive
on how
the ocean breathes.
Believe
when I say
people can
be the ocean
too.

RANDY MASCORRO

If I fell

into myself

would I remember

what this was

and who

my battles

danced with?

And if the hours

were silent

could time

light a match

and set

all that I am

on fire?

We slowly burn.

We slowly

burn.

A MAD SEA

Remind me again
how time stays?
Do we plead and beg
for ourselves
so we can truly see
what is never there?
Do we open our veins up
while everything
we
are to each other
spills out?

RANDY MASCORRO

Tell me about
all those times
you wanted to die,
and I will tell
you
how death
parked their
fucking car
in my body
and never
left.
Can we laugh
while explaining
something sad,
and shiver at
the thought
that we
may never
find it?

A MAD SEA

And if

the days

are painful,

close your eyes

to remember

how the dark

keeps you close.

Rest your worries

for a moment,

rest your voice.

It must be painful

to speak with

so many

wounds.

Beyond everything,
I love you.
Beyond time
and miles,
and the troubles
we grasp.
I love you
for everything
you are not.
People can love someone
for everything they are.
What about everything
they aren't?
The ocean still moves.
The birds still make
their home in the sky.

A MAD SEA

The sky is a blanket
and we are
underneath it.
Shall we dance?
Can we laugh real loud?
Just the clouds
are staring down
so let's get closer.
We can draw hearts
on the palms
of our
hands.

RANDY MASCORRO

Let it fade.
Let you and I
fall where we should
let the grip
we have
on the world
disappear.
Have our thoughts
become startled?
And now
we scream
at
what could
have
been.

A MAD SEA

All this
will make
sense.
They say
all those
lines of
trouble
will go
straight,
and if I
tear
this laughter
out of my lungs,
can I still feel
warmth?

RANDY MASCORRO

I can lay

who I am

in front of you.

I will find rest.

I can take

these fears

off of me.

Every light from

the sky

will undress.

Every light from

the sky

will undress.

A MAD SEA

Remember

when words

overtook us

and we were

cut

for days?

Remember when

all this

was new?

Our hands

became targets

for false hope

when we

touched

each other.

RANDY MASCORRO

In my own worry
I have found
many roads
that still hear me.
Don't you know
these
thoughts still
linger and breathe?
If I ever seem to love you
too much
remember all this was
done before,
and our history
is still alive
in
my eyes.

A MAD SEA

I have bled
tomorrow.
I have
loved you.
Right now,
I have
memorized
your hope
that still
sings
to me
and all my scars
that taste
like
reality.

RANDY MASCORRO

In my

own

blurriness

I have

seen you

when blood

seems like

it won't move.

Remember

that you and I

were proof

that bodies

can scream

like

ocean currents.

A MAD SEA

I have seen

silence

echo

in my eyes.

Tremors of hope

found its way

into my bones.

Maybe it was

words.

Maybe it was

fragments

of myself

that I never

could

grab

hold

of

RANDY MASCORRO

My eyes
are flickering.
Too much
confusion
are words
that fall
to the ground.
My voice hurts.
I haven't
said much.
Silence lingers
until it erupts.
Silence lingers
until it
erupts.

A MAD SEA

Now,
I have never
made peace
with my mind.
Others
have battled
it before.
What I do know
is this.
A scar
and this life
is one.
Words can
shift in our blood.
Chapters keep
us awake.
We bend
who we are
just to reach the end,
not knowing
that every fucking
sentence
passed through.

RANDY MASCORRO

Everything hurts
from the ground up,
and we are taught
to live and forget.
Ignore spills
that become feelings
while wiping away
any truth left
in our voice.
This world
is a constant reminder
everything spins.
We keep silent
when the real racket
spreads in the mind.
It is true,
everything hurts
from the ground up.

A MAD SEA

I realized
that happiness
came from within,
that even water
eventually smiled.
Haven't you ever
seen the ocean
on a bright day?
We run this life
with not enough fuel.
We chase empty
finish lines,
we chase empty
finish lines.

RANDY MASCORRO

If all this
quiet becomes loud
would we hear it?
If all our words
fell to the pavement
would we pick them up?
And if seconds
no longer fucked
the minutes,
would we exist?
The night shouts.
Every demon runs away,
but
we stay,
we stay.

A MAD SEA

My eyes are hurting.

My voice

is not the same.

My mind is twirling.

My hands are cold.

Pain becomes a muse.

Our troubles become

silent.

They rage with no home.

They fall apart

and scatter.

They fall apart

and scatter.

RANDY MASCORRO

Be awake
with me.
Let's be visible
to the stars.
We can pack
everything up
and make this road
a home.
Be here
with me,
know that
our eyes
have seen
each other
before.
Be love
with me,
this life
is a caravan
and we,
we are
traveling
full speed.

A MAD SEA

Whatever it is
with the waters
inside me
always know
I have been swimming
with no destination.
For all these years
whatever it is
between us and our lives
always know
the road ends
with you,
and whatever is hidden
between darkness
and light,
that's what I hope
to become.

RANDY MASCORRO

My eyes scatter
and put themselves
back in place
just so I can see
our lives become locked,
tucked away under lights.
Have I really breathed today?
Have I forgiven myself for
carrying too much?
All the straps will break.
Every burden points a finger.
The dam will scream open.
My life will appear
at your feet.

A MAD SEA

Climb down
from the stars.
They tell me
get out of that daze
and shake reality's hand.
I won't give you
the pleasure.
I will stay up
with the night,
I will climb
constellations
and whisper ideas
to my novels.

RANDY MASCORRO

Silence
and my heart
are miles
apart.
My eyes
and vision
rattle so loud
the door shakes.
My thinking
is now polluted
with music
I can't turn off.
I'll strip myself
empty.
I will show
the night
even the barest
souls
can walk away
unscratched.

A MAD SEA

Take what I have said,
hold on to it.
Breathe this memory.
Question my sanity.
We are just stories
unpaved roads
and unfinished
drawings.

RANDY MASCORRO

She makes me want to scream
my fucking heart out.
Scrounge through the present
and wrestle with the past
wounds
left by those prior.

A MAD SEA

Rip it apart.
Rip apart
what you think of me.
Shred what you thought
yesterday,
and burn every idea.
Sit with me
Let us spill right now.
Let us stare right now
in the eyes.
Let us gather our laughs.
Every second we are new,
Every second we are new.

RANDY MASCORRO

I haven't
been myself.
The sky fell apart
and filled my eyes
with stars.
I curse
at my heart,
and stomp
on these wounds.
I am day drunk,
night lost.

A MAD SEA

We have been
fighting these questions,
but
they are still
visible on this skin.
Stand in the night
with me.
Let darkness
reveal
highways
and these fragments
of our lives
will become novels
hidden away
behind
the sky.

RANDY MASCORRO

Be here now
let us burn
memories in
this bed.
Fingers can
write music
on skin,
and our eyes
can be loud
as an orchestra
sometimes.
I swear,
this is where
we should be
blessed by the sun,
envied by the dark.

A MAD SEA

I have fought enough
with the days.
I have thrown
empty words
into the sky.
This journey
never doubted me.
I could not wash
away the years
even if I tried.
Don't you see?
I am splatered with loss
and
have been stabbed by grief,
but
God dammit
this is how
I breathe.

And sometimes

the sea is

all you have.

Endless water

is endless understanding.

Do not think those waves

do not hear you,

they do.

Keep in mind

they are fighting

battles

just like

us.

A MAD SEA

If you ever

need to hear

my soul

think of the ocean,

let it remind you

that veins

carry stories,

and these eyes

aren't ever quiet.

RANDY MASCORRO

I am done

soul

searching.

The winter air

has heard all

my lies,

the night

is crushing

the sky.

Bare and empty

we shatter in

an instant.

Our laughs

become penniless.

A MAD SEA

I have gave
myself enough.
My eyes struggle
to stay open.
What else can I see?
I guess it is okay
to wrap yourself
in darkness
when the days
won't keep
you warm anymore.

RANDY MASCORRO

Let's go grab food
from that food cart;
the little one you like.
Sidewalks are damp
so all the leaves
look bright.
Let's walk over them
under all the city lights.
We can get lost
even for the day,
or for an hour,
or for the night.

Randy Mascorro is a writer from Hillsboro, Oregon. He contributed two writings to Paradox issue one and "Oceans, Floods and The Sun" will be his debut book with Rad Press Publishing. He's an intense lover of music and his favorite band is The Beatles.

www.ingramcontent.com/pod-product-compliance
Lightning Source LLC
Chambersburg PA
CBHW032048290426
44110CB00012B/1007